Dump Trucks

by Charles Lennie

ABDO
CONSTRUCTION MACHINES
Kids

Visit us at www.abdopublishing.com

Published by Abdo Kids, a division of ABDO, P.O. Box 398166, Minneapolis, Minnesota 55439.

Printed in the United States of America, North Mankato, Minnesota.

032014

092014

 PRINTED ON RECYCLED PAPER

Photo Credits: iStock, Shutterstock, Thinkstock

Production Contributors: Teddy Borth, Jennie Forsberg, Grace Hansen

Design Contributors: Dorothy Toth, Renée LaViolette, Laura Rask

Library of Congress Control Number: 2013952541

Cataloging-in-Publication Data

Lennie, Charles.

 Dump trucks / Charles Lennie.

   p. cm. -- (Construction machines)

ISBN 978-1-62970-018-2 (lib. bdg.)

Includes bibliographical references and index.

1. Dump trucks--Juvenile literature. 2. Construction equipment--Juvenile literature.   I. Title.

629.225--dc23

                      2013952541

Table of Contents

Dump Trucks

Dump trucks are very important. They make certain **tasks** easier.

Dump Truck Parts

The driver sits in the cab. The dumping bed is behind the cab.

dumping bed   **cab**

Using a Dump Truck

The driver controls the dumping bed. The dumping bed holds the **load**.

The dumping bed lifts up

to pour the **load** out.

11

Dump trucks are built **tough**.

They can carry heavy **loads**

from one place to another.

Dump trucks bring

materials like sand or

rocks to construction sites.

14

Dump trucks can help with clean up too! They can carry **waste** away from building sites.

Different Kinds

There are different kinds of dump trucks. Most tilt up and down. Some tilt side to side.

There are giant dump trucks too. They can hold over 380 tons (344,730 kg). That is the same as over 70 elephants!

More Facts

- Dump trucks are used to spread gravel over new roads.

- There are dump trucks made for the winter season. They move snow and spread salt to keep road conditions safe.

- The biggest dump truck does not ever leave the construction site, except in pieces. It is too big to drive on a normal road. So it must be transported and put together once it makes it to the site.

Glossary

cab – where the driver sits to control the machine.

load – the total amount that can be carried.

material – matter from which a thing is or can be made.

tasks – pieces of work to be done.

tough – strong.

waste – material that is no longer useful.

Index

abdokids.com

Use this code to log on to abdokids.com and access crafts, games, videos and more!

Abdo Kids Code:
CDK0182